Little Frog's Tadpole Trouble

by

Tatyana Feeney

OXFORD

UNIVERSITY PRESS

Little Frog lived with his
Mummy and Daddy.
It was just the three of them.

Two

plus one.

And Little Frog
liked it that way.

One day Mummy and Daddy
told Little Frog that he was
going to be a big brother . . .

to nine baby tadpoles!

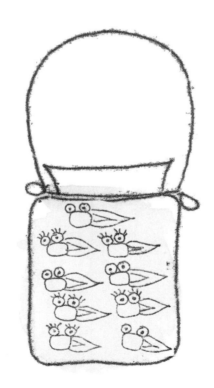

Little Frog was **not** impressed.

The tadpoles couldn't
build a tower.

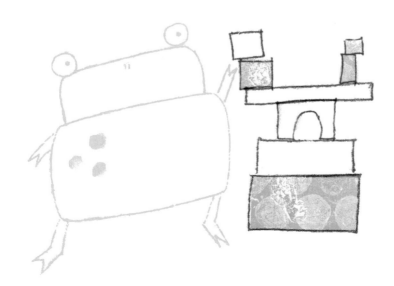

The tadpoles couldn't
play the drums.

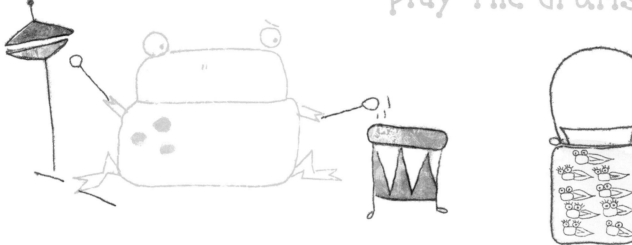

The tadpoles couldn't
even jump.

They didn't do anything...

except take up **all** of
Mummy's and Daddy's time.

When Little Frog wanted
his bedtime story . . .

Mummy was too busy.

When Little Frog wanted
his goodnight kiss . . .

Daddy was too busy.

'Silly tadpoles,' said Little Frog.

'Well,' said Daddy, 'you were once a tadpole too, and very soon they will be little frogs . . .

. . . just like you.'

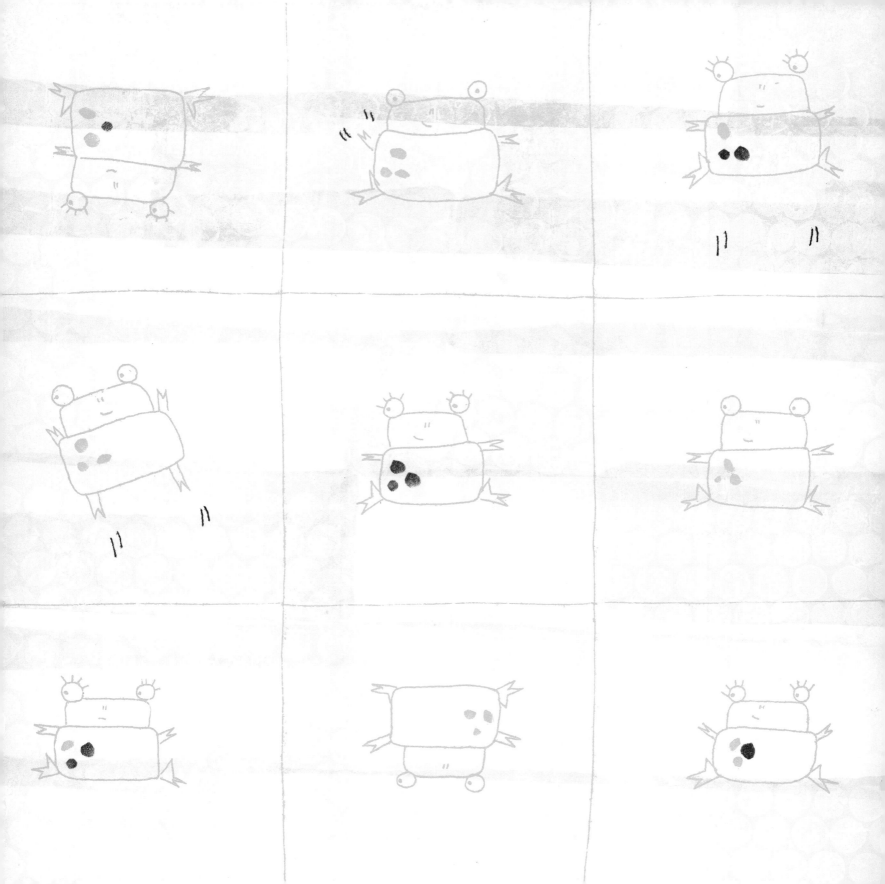

Little Frog could do all
sorts of things with his
brothers and sisters.

In particular
building rather
good towers.

So now his family was
two plus one
plus nine new playmates.

And Little Frog was the
best big brother to them all.

To Fionn, my first tadpole and the best big brother

OXFORD
UNIVERSITY PRESS

Great Clarendon Street, Oxford OX2 6DP

Oxford University Press is a department of the University of Oxford.
It furthers the University's objective of excellence in research, scholarship,
and education by publishing worldwide in

Oxford   New York

Auckland Cape Town Dar es Salaam Hong Kong Karachi
Kuala Lumpur Madrid Melbourne Mexico City Nairobi
New Delhi Shanghai Taipei Toronto

With offices in

Argentina Austria Brazil Chile Czech Republic France Greece
Guatemala Hungary Italy Japan Poland Portugal Singapore
South Korea Switzerland Thailand Turkey Ukraine Vietnam

Oxford is a registered trade mark of Oxford University Press
in the UK and in certain other countries

Text and illustrations © Tatyana Feeney 2014

The moral rights of the author/illustrator have been asserted

Database right Oxford University Press (maker)

First published in 2014

British Library Cataloguing in Publication Data available

ISBN: 978-0-19-273554-6 (hardback)
ISBN: 978-0-19-273555-3 (paperback)

2 4 6 8 10 9 7 5 3 1

Printed in China

Paper used in the production of this book is a natural,
recyclable product made from wood grown in sustainable forests.
The manufacturing process conforms to the environmental
regulations of the country of origin